TIME FOR KIDS®

DEVELOPING READER 2 — Science Scoops

Earthquakes!

By the Editors of TIME FOR KIDS
WITH BARBARA COLLIER

HarperCollinsPublishers

About the Author: Barbara Collier works as a copy editor for TIME magazine and as a freelance writer and editor for other publications, including TIME FOR KIDS®. She has traveled along the San Andreas Fault in California and is planning a trip to Valdivia, Chile, near the site of the 1960 earthquake.

To Noah, whose curiosity about the natural world sparked my own.

Thanks to those who shared their expertise: Lisa Wald of the United States Geological Survey; John Rutherford, founder, and Bret Lizundia and Mark Saunders, principals, of the engineering firm Rutherford and Chekene in Oakland, California. —B.C.

Earthquakes!
Copyright © 2006 by Time Inc.
Used under exclusive license by HarperCollins Publishers Inc.
Manufactured in China.

Library of Congress Cataloging-in-Publication Data is available.

ISBN-10: 0-06-078211-0 (pbk.) — ISBN-10: 0-06-078212-9 (trade)
ISBN-13: 978-0-06-078211-5 (pbk.) — ISBN-13: 978-0-06-078212-2 (trade)

1 2 3 4 5 6 7 8 9 10
First Edition

Photography and Illustration Credits:
Cover: Ruaridh Stewart—Zuma Press; cover insert: Patrick Aventurier—Gamma; cover front flap: Kimimasa Mayama—Reuters; title page: Wang Yuan-mao—AP; contents page: Roger Ressmeyer—Corbis; pp. 4–5: Atta Kenare—AFP/Getty Images; pp. 6–9: Lon Tweeten; pp. 10–11: Mike Lisowski—USGS/AP; pp. 12–13: Simon Kwong—Reuters; pg. 12 (inset): AP; pp. 14–15: Paul A. Souders—Corbis; pg. 14 (inset): Myrleen Ferguson Cate—PhotoEdit; pp. 16–17: Joanne Davis—AFP/Getty Images; pp. 18–19: Bullit Marquez—AP; pp. 20–21: Craig Aurness—Corbis; pg. 21 (inset): Joe Lertola; pp. 22–23: Corbis; pp. 24–25: Lloyd Cluff—Corbis; pg. 24 (inset): Corbis; pp. 26–27: Mark L. Stephenson—Corbis; pp. 28–29: PMEL Tsunami Research Program/NOAA; pg. 28 (inset): NOAA/AP; pp. 30–31: Yoshikazu Tsuno—AFP/Getty Images; pg. 31 (inset): Jim Sugar—Corbis; pg. 32 (epicenter): Corbis; pg. 32 (fault line): Lon Tweeten; pg. 32 (focus): Lon Tweeten; pg. 32 (landslide): Lloyd Cluff—Corbis; pg. 32 (plate): Lon Tweeten; pg. 32 (tsunami): Joanne Davis—AFP/Getty Images; pg. 32 (fun fact): John Courtney

Acknowledgments:
For TIME FOR KIDS: Editorial Director: Keith Garton; Editor: Nelida Gonzalez Cutler; Art Director: Rachel Smith; Designer: Susan Low; Photography Editor: Jill Tatara

 Check us out at www.timeforkids.com

CONTENTS

San Francisco, California,
after the 1989 quake

CHAPTER ONE

The Earth

Rocks!

The destruction
from a 2003
quake in
Bam, Iran

Rumble! The ground is shaking.
It is an earthquake!
Earthquakes happen every day.
Most of them are gentle.
But big quakes can make buildings
fall down.

The Seven Big Plates

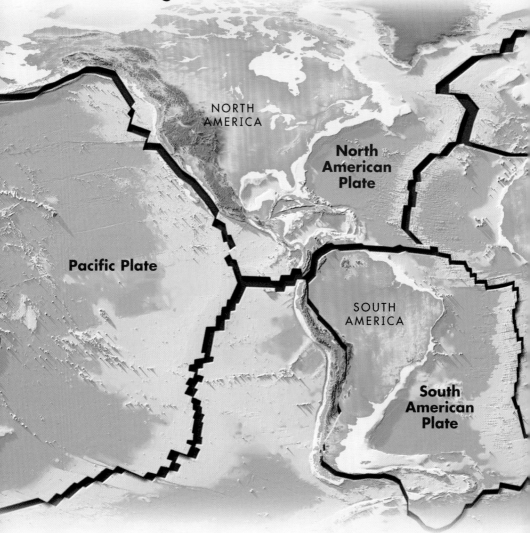

NORTH
AMERICA

**North
American
Plate**

Pacific Plate

SOUTH
AMERICA

**South
American
Plate**

What makes the earth shake?

The earth's top layer, or crust, is like a jigsaw puzzle.
It has seven big pieces and some smaller pieces.

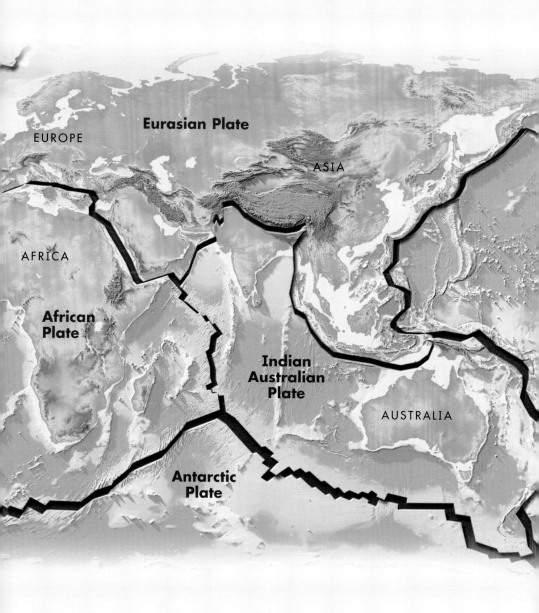

EUROPE

Eurasian Plate

ASIA

AFRICA

African Plate

Indian Australian Plate

AUSTRALIA

Antarctic Plate

The pieces of crust are called plates.
They move a little bit all the time.
They move so slowly that we never even feel it.

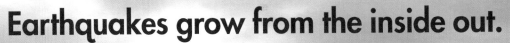

Earthquakes grow from the inside out.

Sometimes two plates bump together underground.
They might slip past each other.
Or one might slide under the other.
Energy is released and travels up to the surface.
Everything on the ground shakes.

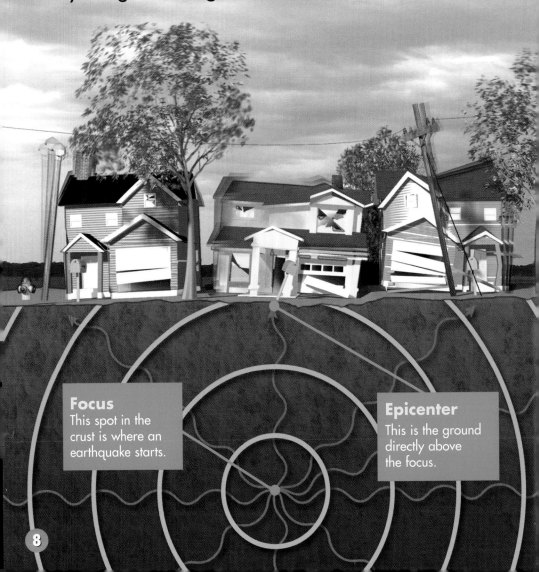

Focus
This spot in the crust is where an earthquake starts.

Epicenter
This is the ground directly above the focus.

Inside the Earth

Take a look inside the earth to find out what makes the plates move.

Inner Core
A ball of solid metal is at the center of the earth.

Outer Core
A layer of burning-hot melted rock lies above the inner core.

Mantle
Hot, dense rock flows slowly here.

Crust
This is the earth's surface layer. It is broken into plates that float above the mantle.

Fault Line
This is the place where two plates meet. Many earthquakes happen here.

Energy Waves
They carry the force of the earthquake and cause damage on the surface.

CHAPTER TWO

Measuring

Can you tell when a quake will hit?
Scientists are trying to find out.
They study the earth's movements.
Often smaller quakes come before
a big earthquake.
These are called foreshocks.

Movement

A scientist in Washington near Mount St. Helens

Spotlight

In 1935 Charles Richter found
a way to measure quakes.
He used a machine called
a seismograph.
It draws wiggly lines to show how
much motion happens in a quake.
Richter gave each quake a number.
An earthquake that measures 1
on the Richter scale is very weak.
One that measures more than 7 is strong.
Today scientists use different scales to measure
the magnitude, or strength, of a quake.

A researcher with
a seismograph

Scientists learn from history.

They study quakes that happened long ago.
They also look at quakes that happen now.
Maybe someday they will be able to tell
when an earthquake will strike.

A barking
dog

Can animals sense that an earthquake is coming?

Scientists cannot prove that they do.
But sometimes animals act strangely
before an earthquake hits.
Birds fly in circles.
Dogs bark for hours.
Elephants start to run.

Elephants in
Sri Lanka

CHAPTER THREE

Monster Quakes

Many earthquakes happen under
the ocean floor.
Ocean waves can form after a quake.
They grow bigger near the shore.
Then they crash.
This is called a tsunami (soo-NAH-mee),
or wall of water.

A tsunami hit
Thailand in 2004.

A village in Indonesia after the 2004 tsunami

A large tsunami hit South Asia in 2004.

Powerful waves wiped out villages. There were more than 174,000 victims. People from all over the world sent money and supplies to help.

Many earthquakes happen around the Pacific Ocean.
This area is known as the Ring of Fire.
California is in the Ring of Fire.
This state has the 750-mile-long
San Andreas Fault.
Thousands of quakes occur here
every year.

ASIA

NORTH
AMERICA

PACIFIC OCEAN

SOUTH
AMERICA

AUSTRALIA

The Ring of Fire

**The San
Andreas Fault
in California**

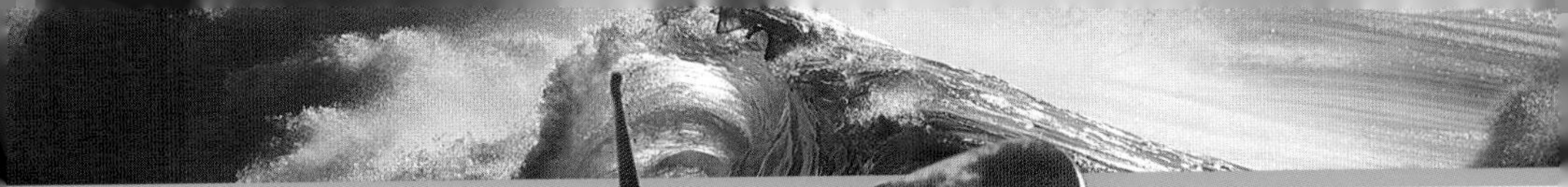

PIONEER
AR
D&D
CAFE
LOANS
TV
SHOW
ARCADE
OPEN 24 HRS
SCANDINAVIAN CLUB-BAR
PAWN SHOP
LOANS
AMUSEMENTS
PIONEER LOAN CO.
ANS
LOANS
WE SHIP
COD
Expert
JEWELRY AND
WATCH REPAIR

A huge earthquake shook Alaska in 1964.
It measured a magnitude 9.2. That was the biggest earthquake ever recorded in the United States!

Anchorage, Alaska, after the 1964 quake

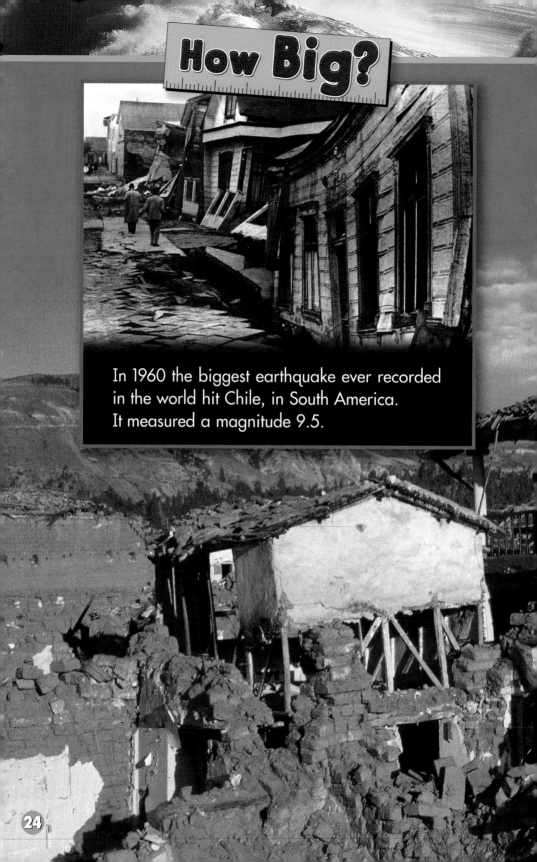

How Big?

In 1960 the biggest earthquake ever recorded in the world hit Chile, in South America. It measured a magnitude 9.5.

After a 1970
landslide in Peru

Watch out below!

An earthquake can cause an avalanche
or a landslide.
Snow, rocks, and mud start to move.
They come crashing down a mountain!

CHAPTER FOUR

Stay Safe!

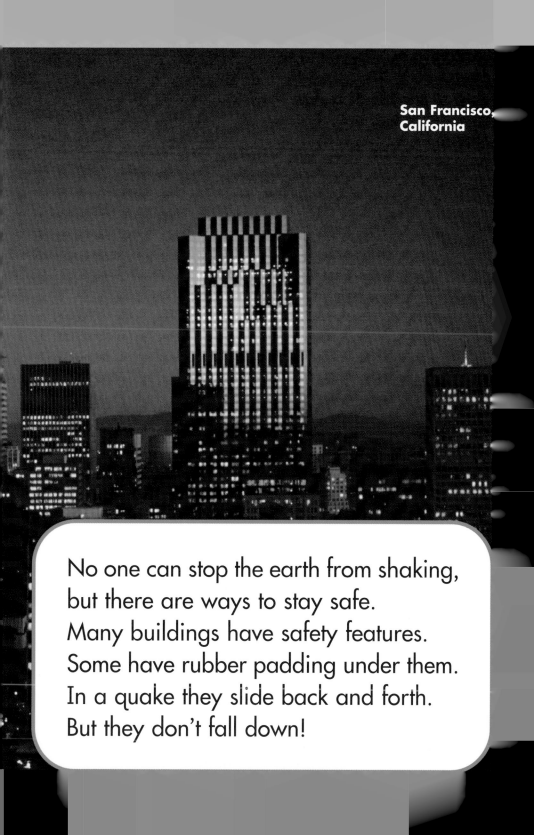

San Francisco, California

No one can stop the earth from shaking,
but there are ways to stay safe.
Many buildings have safety features.
Some have rubber padding under them.
In a quake they slide back and forth.
But they don't fall down!

The tsunami warning system alerts people to danger.
Scientists measure changes in
the sea level.
They look for signs of possible trouble.
When a warning goes out,
move away from the shore!

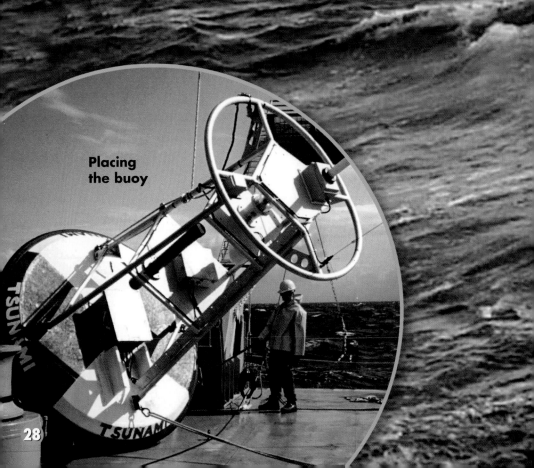

Placing
the buoy

28

A warning buoy in the Pacific Ocean

What to Do in a Quake

☒ If you are outside, move away
from power lines, trees, and buildings.

☒ If you are inside, stay away from windows, mirrors,
cupboards, and shelves.

☒ Take cover under a heavy table or desk.
Hold on to it.

☒ Be prepared for possible shaking after the main quake.
These shakes are called aftershocks.

☒ Most important, stay calm.

**An earthquake
drill in Japan**

Did You Know?

 In 1755 an earthquake hit Lisbon, Portugal. The energy waves were so huge that people in colonial America could feel them.

 There are volcanoes along some of the same fault lines as earthquakes.

 Every year more than three million small earthquakes shake the world! Only about eighteen measure more than a magnitude 7.

 An earthquake's energy waves travel fifteen times as fast as a jet plane.

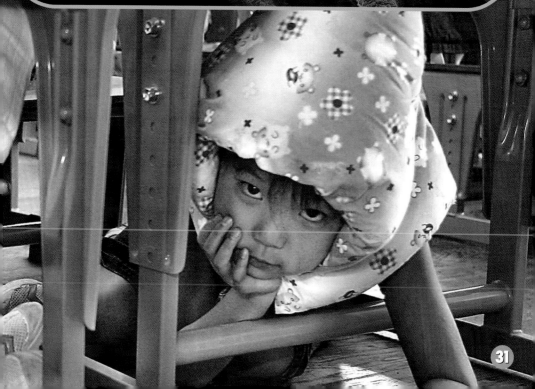

A volcano in Hawaii erupted in 1984.

WORDS to Know

Epicenter: the ground directly above the focus of a quake

Landslide: the movement of earth, mud, and rocks down a mountain

Fault line: the place where two plates meet

Plate: a piece of the earth's crust

Focus: the spot in the earth's crust where a quake starts

Tsunami: huge waves from an undersea earthquake that crash on shore

FUN FACT

Two thousand years ago, a Chinese scientist recorded earthquakes. He used a big jar with dragons and toads on the sides. When a ball fell out of a dragon's mouth into a toad's mouth, he knew an earthquake was happening!